Getting Organized

Other Classmates

2nd Series

1st Series

Getting Organized

Angela Thody and Derek Bowden

continuum
LONDON • NEW YORK

Continuum

The Tower Building
11 York Road
London SE1 7NX
www.continuumbooks.com

15 East 26th Street
New York
NY 10010

First published 2004

British Library Cataloguing-in-Publication Data
A catalogue record for this book is available from the British Library.

ISBN 0-8264-6770-9

Typeset by Originator Publishing Services, Gt Yarmouth
Printed and bound by Antony Rowe Ltd., Chippenham, Wiltshire

Contents

Contents

About the Authors

Angela Thody is Professor of Educational Leadership at the International Institute for Education Leadership (IIEL), University of Lincoln. Angela has taught every age group from 3 to 83-year-olds, and currently leads the doctoral programmes at the IIEL for senior leaders in education. Her teaching career began with the 16+ age group before extending into higher education. While taking a career break for family development, she freelanced in playgroups, primary and secondary schools, and adult education. Angela has researched and published extensively, including six books, some 50 articles and numerous conference presentations. She is invited to lecture world-wide on teaching issues and was the first female president of the Commonwealth Council for Educational Administration and Management 1994–2000.

Derek Bowden is course leader for the MBA in International Educational Leadership at the International Leadership Centre, University of Hull. He spent 32 years teaching in schools, and his final post was head of a comprehensive school in Cheshire for 13 years. Before taking up his lectureship at Hull, he taught in masters programmes with the Open University and the universities of Lincoln and Leicester. He has worked extensively as a consultant for LEAs and schools. In recent years the focus of this work has been directed towards developing whole-school approaches to dealing with the pressures on heads and staff.

Introduction

The following pages offer rapid, readable and practical guidance to help increase your success in managing:

♦ your time;

♦ the possible stress factors in your job;

♦ your career development in teaching;

♦ your move to an alternative career using the skills acquired in teaching.

Each section takes about fifteen minutes to read, has practical examples and offers self-review activities to make what you have read personal to you.

'There is a danger of seeing a 50+ hour week as a mark of noble dedication to the cause of education.'

1

Time Management

Using time well – life outside teaching

Teaching is a busy, hectic and pressurized job. Work is not confined to time in school and you spend doubtless many hours at home on schoolwork. This isn't necessarily a bad thing if you are enjoying it; but there is a danger of seeing a 50+ hour week as a mark of noble dedication to the cause of education.

Perhaps working long hours does reflect commitment, but it can also mean that you miss out on personal and leisure activities. Over the years this can reduce the 'buzz' you bring to the classroom. You can become adequate rather than inspirational. The psychologically-tired teacher is the one more vulnerable to stress.

So would you like an evening with three to four hours' free of schoolwork? Start by using the quiz (Figure 1) to identify your personal *time-thieves*.

If you have checked 'Always' against every statement then you don't need this section. If, however, you have options marked in the other columns, consider which of them you could move at least one column to the left. That's the first move towards saving time on work tasks so that you can recycle it as personal, family, leisure or home time (your personal agenda), and towards making more effective use of

Getting Organized

	Always	Usually	Sometimes	Rarely
1. I make and use a weekly plan.				
2. I am clear about more long-term tasks that need doing.				
3. I create blocks of time for big jobs.				
4. I deal with interruptions effectively in school.				
5. I deal with interruptions effectively at home.				
6. I deal with paperwork efficiently.				
7. I can find things in school.				
8. I can find things at home.				
9. I keep on top of marking.				
10. I have organized times for preparation.				
11. Informal meetings are short and focused.				
12. Discussions with colleagues are to the point.				
13. Formal meetings in school are well run.				
14. I use other people well.				
15. Senior managers in school seem to respect my time.				
16. The school has efficient systems for routine information.				
17. I find time to relax out of school.				
18. I programme and maintain my leisure activities.				
19. Even when under pressure I feel in control of the day.				

Figure 1. Identify your time thieves.

work time by prioritizing tasks (your professional agenda).

The bad news is that to recycle your time, you are going to have to change the way you do things. That

'The bad news is that to recycle your time, you are going to have to change the way you do things. That can be uncomfortable in the short run.'

can be uncomfortable in the short run. However, the good news is that it really does work: which brings long-term comfort. Finally, the helpful news is that teams and whole school staffs can collectively attack time management.

The potential benefits are enormous. We recommend that school senior managers accept the key responsibility for ensuring that their staff operate in a time-efficient environment. The starting point for this is to score the statements together to create a *team agenda*. Ways of dealing with this agenda are described in the rest of this section.

Time management is more difficult (but more necessary) if you have family or domestic commitments. Young children are premier league time-thieves, and ironing, cleaning, etc. need planned slots. The heavier the commitments, the more important your organization of personal time becomes (see Figure 2).

Organize your time

Rule 1: Take control of interruptions

Dealing with a class demands total concentration, which means any interruption of precious non-contact time becomes even more costly to your planning. Interruptions can come from colleagues, children, parents and other professionals. There are numerous ways of responding to interruptions. For example: you have one hour free and intend to use this time to start writing end-of-year reports on pupils. These are due in 10 days' time but you have very little free time between now

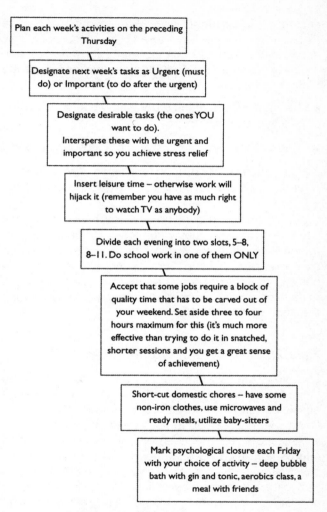

Figure 2. Planning your week.

and then. A colleague says 'Glad to get the chance to talk to you – we have to arrange those appraisals and I need information on Waynetta for the exclusion meeting next week'. Which of these replies would you make?

♦ 'I've got to finish these reports now but I can see you at break/after school.'

♦ 'Can't really help right now – rushed off my feet!'

♦ 'OK, appraisal first then exclusion. Let's wrap it up in ten minutes, then I'm starting these reports.'

When deciding on a response, you have to balance your needs and priorities with those of your colleagues. It is remarkable how, within a time-aware staff, these assertive responses do not cause offence and the number of interruptions is reduced. It is also possible to develop a similar strategy at home, particularly when the task needs a block of time.

Rule 2: Take control of paperwork

Sort your mail/pigeonhole/tray daily into junk to be binned, trivia to be dealt with quickly (immediately if possible), and important items requiring attention. Don't give equal value to each piece of paper.

At school the management of paper and routine information needs careful thought. A cluttered, rarely-cleared noticeboard is actually a barrier to efficient communication. A named person must be responsible for any staffroom system. Larger schools find a five-minute morning briefing very useful – as long as it is

'A cluttered, rarely-cleared noticeboard is actually a barrier to efficient communication.'

properly planned and conducted. Smaller schools can use a whiteboard in the staffroom with colour coding for topics and/or people.

It is good practice for senior managers who distribute Local Education Authority (LEA), Department for Education and Employment (DfEE) and similar documents to reduce each one to a single A4 side of key points, with the original kept available for reference. If bulky documents are just passed on they will not be read. This will only work, however, if staff accept their part of the deal and read the key points.

Rule 3: Take control of your filing and storage

To begin with we need to analyse the kind of person you are. Are you:

♦ the *non-filer* ('I know I put it somewhere safe/in this pile/on that chair');

♦ the *hoarder* ('I chuck everything in that box – at least I know I've got it');

♦ the *obsessive* ('I sort everything into classifications, have a box for each when pending, a box for each when completed and then I file all paperwork. I keep everything'):

♦ the *office manager* ('I keep only what needs to be kept and have a regular (termly) clear-out. Most of it is electronically filed')?

Which *should* you be? Don't rush to assume that you ought to be the office manager type. The authors have worked with people in all the categories. Some manage to be efficient whichever system they adopt; others flounder in stress, struggling to find important records even within what appears to be a well-organized filing cabinet.

Organize your filing and storage system so that it:

♦ suits you (you can remember where things are and can access them quickly);

♦ fits your method of working (clear out once a term, a year, or when moving jobs);

♦ provides you with enough security that you have retained all necessary documents;

♦ is within your competence (if you're not computer literate, then electronic filing is not for you);

♦ meets the needs of colleagues (they don't want their work delayed by your inability to find materials).

Rule 4: Take control of your marking and preparation

Our experience is that many teachers feel guilty about marking and preparation because they feel they could always do more but there are simply not enough hours in the day.

The purpose of marking is to record achievement and to give useful feedback. Increasingly, schools are developing homework and marking policies which highlight the necessity of relevant tasks as well as clear learning objectives (ideally explained to the class). Marking should focus on these objectives. It is

'A common scenario sees a few people doing most of the talking, with an apparently passive or apathetic audience. Afterwards, in the staff car park, people who have been silent for over an hour break into animated discussion about the meeting.'

a sensible professional strategy to accept that some things will be done to a two- or three-star rather than a four-star level. Managers should bring this into the open so there is guilt-free dialogue about fairness, priorities and workload; this can prevent the current exploitation by the system of the goodwill (and fear?) of industrious teachers.

To cope with our own marking, we have found the advice given in Figure 3 useful.

Rule 5: Take control of meetings

Most staff meetings take place at the end of the teaching (not working) day. A common scenario sees a few people doing most of the talking, with an apparently passive or apathetic audience. Afterwards, in the staff car park, people who have been silent for over an hour break into animated discussion about the meeting.

We are concerned that the meeting process fails to channel and utilize this energy and interest. The danger for a young teacher is to assume 'that's the way meetings have to be'. You might feel powerless to improve meetings in your school, but there are aspects the individual can affect. In the following discussion note what *you* can do and what needs to be done by senior management.

First, reflect on what you think are unproductive meetings at your school. How much of the inefficiency do you think is due to the following?

♦ Meetings lack a clear and generally understood purpose.

Pupils' needs	Your needs
Aims of marking	
A sense of achievement.	Awareness of your pupils' progress/difficulties.
Useful feedback on how far they have reached the learning objectives.	Avoidance of exposure to the criticisms of well-intentioned but ill-informed parents who feel that insufficient marking is being done.
Some indication of the importance of their standards of literacy or numeracy so that they are aware that these matter in all subjects.	Ensuring you have enough information for report writing.
Rapid return of marked work.	Avoidance of exhaustion from trying to keep up with all the marking.
How to mark	
Reduce the red – a mass of comments is demoralizing and the pupil will learn nothing.	Check that you are marking in accord with the school's policies on feedback.
Don't correct every error – it doesn't help the pupil to avoid repeating them.	Indicate that you have seen each piece of work done by your pupils – even it is only ticked and dated or has a brief comment.
Mark only part of the work for standards of literacy or numeracy; explain why you are including these cross-curricular issues and that your comments are to give an indication of where improvements might be made.	Don't mark every error.
Include positive comments and ticks as well as critical marking.	Keep records of your marks.
	Feel positive about having completed one pile of marking, rather than negative about the other four piles still to be done.
	Be aware that marking is to help pupils feel good and to learn; it is not done for senior managers, bureaucracy or OFSTED.

Figure 2 Aims of marking

- Meetings are too long.

- Agendas are too full, consisting of a list of items rather than a framework for discussion.

- Too many people are present.

- Meetings are run (chaired) by the most senior person present.

- Meetings are adversarial in style, high on structure and formal procedure, low on creativity.

- Minutes of the previous meeting are a nit-picker's paradise, concentrating on the past rather than the present or future.

Each of these problems is discussed below along with possible solutions.

Clear purpose

Problem

Many schools are locked into a pattern of meetings, which is decided a year in advance. There are good reasons for this, including the need for people to arrange their diaries. The problem is that the rigidity of structure and, particularly in secondary schools, the various structural levels at which matters are discussed, preclude a fast, incisive response to the unpredictable year ahead. Programmed meetings tend to be held even if not needed. Is there really value in eight different departmental meetings, each discussing boys' discipline? The typical secondary system is so

'Programmed meetings tend to be held even if not needed. Is there really value in eight different departmental meetings, each discussing boys' discipline?'

ponderous that the intended flow of ideas up and down the structure is often overtaken by events. We still know schools where staff have to attend meetings to ensure their 1265 hours are accounted for. This is a punitive policy which has a negative effect on the good-will which is the lifeblood of staff relations.

Solution

Replace this structure-driven system with a number of small, focused task-groups dealing with specific issues from the school development plan in a short time-frame. The authority of these groups to make decisions or recommendations to senior management must be clearly defined.

Length of meetings

Problem

Expecting people to contribute usefully for more than one hour after a day's teaching is unrealistic.

Solution

Make one hour the maximum meeting length and try, using techniques given in this section, to reduce this to 30 minutes.

Agendas

Problem

These tend to contain too many items, forming an

unhappy mix of routine administration and deep educational issues. Neither area is adequately addressed and items late in the agenda are rushed through or carried over. Each item on the agenda is given as a single word or short phrase, for example 'end-of-term arrangements'.

Let us review what this item will be about from the point of view of six people attending the meeting. They might have seen the agenda previously or, as is more likely, have been given it at the meeting.

Andrew:
'This is about closing an hour early like last year.'
Betty:
'This is about having class parties.'
Clive:
'This is about extra supervision at break.'
Donna:
'This is about clearing displays off the walls.'
Edwin:
'This is about having all records up-to-date.'
Fiona:
'This is about having a collective psychological closure to promote community spirit.'

Six people will be (partly) prepared for quite different discussions, each of them valid. All might be different from the convenor's intentions.

Solution

An active agenda format (see Figure 4).

The agenda should be issued to all participants and displayed in the staffroom (in a dedicated location) for three days before the meeting. It is accepted practice for people with particular interest or concern to consult

Item	Item leader	Purpose	Time
End-of-term arrangements			
(a) Early closure	Andrew	To identify views on pros and cons for recommendations to governors	3 min
(b) Class parties	Betty	To decide by majority for or against	1 min
(c) Break supervision	Clive	To request voluntary staff help for people on duty	1 min
(d) Display clearance	Donna	To confirm site manager's request	30 sec
(e) Class records	Edwin	To confirm details of necessary records and deadlines	1 min
(f) Psychological closure	Fiona	To explain the reasons for and potential value of: • identification of staff views • change of present policy by consensus only	5 min

Figure 4. An active agenda.

the item leader who might then summarize various points as an introduction to the topic. Items (d) and (e) (in Figure 4) are on implementation of policy and will not be discussed (we know that Fred would like to have his usual moan about workload at the end of term but we have heard it all before).

Number of people attending

Problem

As the number attending rises, the dynamics of a meeting change until spectating and even posturing become more frequent. Observe a large meeting and you will see these and other symptoms of dysfunction. It raises the question of *opportunity cost* (what else the spectators could be doing with their time) and *effectiveness* (the toxic effect of inflexible or defensive views expressed and repeated in front of a captive audience).

Solution

Select the number of people according to the purpose of the meeting: 3–6 for explaining ideas and resolving problems; 6–10 for routine management, implementation issues, matters requiring input from particular levels of management; and all staff for quick briefings, bonding or celebrations.

In small primary schools such advice might seem superfluous, but success there lies in restricting the *purpose* of the meeting. With a small staff, it is tempting to have all-purpose meetings which then drag on. Stick to specific purposes and keep the meeting short.

Leading (chairing) the meeting

Problem

Traditionally this is done by the most senior person present, who is also the convenor responsible for the agenda. The same person is probably the most active protagonist, introducing ideas and fielding questions.

Solution

Leading a meeting requires full concentration on the agenda, the participants, and the co-ordination of discussion. The chairing (we prefer the terms 'leading' or 'directing') should be done by a member who has co-ordinating, interpreting and summarizing skills. It is a facilitating role, not an authority/power thing. We suggest that the team leader should (gladly) hand over the responsibility of running the meeting to a colleague. This also sends signals about task-focused collaboration between professionals and reduces the status/power dimension that is common in meetings.

Minutes

Problem

Minutes are time-consuming and can be inaccurate, inadequate, or superfluous. The business of 'minutes of the last meeting' is a mischief-maker's charter which can be used to undermine the present meeting.

'The chairing should be done by a member who has co-ordinating, interpreting and summarizing skills. It is a facilitating role, not an authority/power thing.'

Solution

We suggest replacing minutes by an action report which is attached to the relevant agenda. This report lists decisions, the person responsible for implementing them, the time-scale and people who need to be informed of a particular item outcome. We suggest copies of the action report are given to participants and displayed on a dedicated notice board.

Use other people's time

This could be subtitled 'delegation', except that this essential component of collaborative work has been mis-used by managers who confuse delegation with dumping. Delegation is a short-term contract with clearly defined tasks, outcomes, levels of autonomy and degrees of supervision. Dumping is a single off-loading of work you don't want to do, to someone who can't (or won't) say no.

Delegation, when done well, is a massive time-saver. A number of people working individually or in pairs can achieve so much more than by working together through all the tasks. Traditionally, delegation is done 'downwards' in the hierarchy. We suggest you can also delegate 'upwards' and 'across'.

Upward delegation addresses the complaint about senior management frequently heard in the staffroom: 'Why don't they just do it and tell us?' (The same people will also complain about 'lack of consultation', but you can't win them all.) Upward delegation raises a fundamental philosophical/ethical issue. It involves reducing the amount of consultational participation between senior management and grass-roots staff. The key skill is to reduce the amount, saving many people-hours, but without reducing the level. In this way senior managers can preserve (and even enhance) the notions of professional collaboration and valuing colleagues. It requires skilled selection and communication (and occasionally a thick skin!).

Delegation 'across' is essentially a sharing-out between equals. You can also ask a colleague to do a job because they are particularly good at it, or you can offer or exchange something you will do for them.

Senior managers respecting people's time

A time-intelligent school needs senior managers who use their time well and allow/encourage others to do the same. The personal time available to a busy teacher affects the quality of life. We see skilled time management as an *imperative* for managers.

School improvement gained at the cost of the well-being of teachers is only short term. The key is to work smarter, not harder. Too many teachers and senior managers spend time on administration tasks that could be done by a 16-year-old.

It is the headteacher who ultimately has to take responsibility for many of the strategies suggested in this section. Some of them have serious implications for the traditional ways of working in schools.

The re-engineering of staff consultation and meetings and the notion of *openly* accepting two- and three-star solutions to workload problems all require brave and visionary leadership.

Reward your time

Relaxing out of school – beware the throbbing bag

It's likely that you, like us, take schoolwork home – usually preparation and marking. In recent years teachers' bags have become bigger and bigger. Some people now use crates or boxes and need special lifting techniques to empty the boots of their cars! When you get home the bag sits in a corner or under the stairs. Typically, because you are tired from a hard day, you do something else. Maybe you relax with the family, watch television, or just sit in an exhausted slump. Two hours later the bag is still there and is beginning to send messages to you. To avoid these you may go to the shops, or the pub, or watch television. On your return, the bag is still there, pulsating. It is too late to start working on it now. The bag goes back to school next day with the work still undone. You will not have properly relaxed the previous evening because of the throbbing bag.

Perhaps you can identify with this scenario. If so, what are the solutions?

♦ Use the suggestions in this section and you will need the bag less.

♦ Take only *one* job home.

23

Getting Organized

- ◆ Remember that you have planned the evening in two parts and schoolwork must only be done in one of them.

- ◆ Have at least one evening in the week clear of schoolwork.

Beware joining the ranks of the over-conscientious and unappreciated.

Avoid becoming a victim of the pincer movement between a busy job and other people's needs. Don't feel guilty about prioritizing *your* needs.

When you can't respond immediately to an interruption, you are not being selfish, you are asking people to respect your time as you respect theirs.

It is worth investing short-term time into building your filing and storage system for the long-term gain.

Start using some of the ideas in this section in small departmental or key stage meetings where status is less of an obstacle. Be patient – these ideas require learned skills.

Whether colleagues delegate to you upwards, across, or downwards, seek clarification of the terms of the 'contract'. Remind them not to 'snoopervise'.

At the end of a homework session give yourself a little reward. These are a key part of time management. It can be a walk in the park, listening to a favourite CD with the cat on your lap, half an hour of rubbish television, or a piece of chocolate (the last one has side-effects – be careful). Identify and look forward to your little reward.

'80 million working days in Britain are lost annually to sick leave takers for stress.'

2

Stress Management

You *will* have it all but don't even try to have everything all at once.

The stress argument

Make just one week's trawl through daily newspapers, weekly and monthly magazines for both men and women, and you'll find 'stress' items in every one, with stress perceived as:

♦ a word to use for everything from mild anxiety to severe clinical depression (if you have the latter, don't spend time on this section, go straight to a doctor);

♦ normal for everyone;

♦ particularly suffered by teachers;

♦ always damaging, and we should not be subjected to it;

- preventable with self-help;

- worse now than ever before.

On the other hand, there are the sceptics who feel that stress is just an adult's comfort blanket and it's time we grew up and coped without it. Each of these possibilities is considered below.

Media hype – stress is everywhere

Headlines tell us that 80 million working days in Britain are lost annually to sick leave takers for stress. Did you know that 25 per cent of your colleagues are stressed? Every teacher in your school, including you, is estimated to be taking seven days leave for stress-related illnesses every year (eight and a half days if you are in a primary school).

Stress causes you to lose patience with your work colleagues and pupils, forget appointments and fail to produce reports on time. Homeward bound you'll suffer attacks of road rage or supermarket angst. Once home, you'll shout at your partner and/or fall asleep with no energy to shout.

The media's suggested cures for stress are legion. From vitamins to herbal remedies to manufactured drugs, there is always a pill to help you cope with stress. Alternatively, why not try physical relief mechanisms such as tapping your head with light percussive movements, power sleeping for eight hours, combing your fingers through your hair, or lying down in an enclosed water tank?

If these fail to help you, go and talk with a counsellor, a relative, a friend, someone at the bus stop, your professional development co-ordinator, or even yourself as you stroll up a lonely mountain. Start exercising; swim, row, jump, or run marathons. Take up a new hobby; study, cook or communicate with your family. All should help dissipate your stress.

If you don't have time to fit these in, then use on-site masseurs. These come to your school and chair-massage your stress points. You will be happily back in the work environment within 20 minutes.

If all these remedies fail, sue your employer and/or take early retirement on stress-related grounds. After all, you did not anticipate having to teach subjects that were not your degree specialism. Nor did you expect that pupils might sometimes be difficult to control, or that a parent might be angry with you. Your school should have prevented this happening and then you would not be stressed.

All this stress is apparently only a late twentieth-/early twenty-first-century disease. For teachers, it has been caused by coping with rapid changes in technology, teaching methods, curriculum demands and the higher standards that must be attained.

Stress sceptics – pull yourself together

The sceptics see stress as something that has been over-hyped and with which we should be able to cope. A collection of their views includes:

- It's usual for all of us to worry sometimes, but is it necessary to define this as stress?

- Isn't stress something we all need to give us a 'high' to stimulate action?

- A teacher writing in the education press in 1999 complained that he needed one week of the summer holidays to 'wind down' from work pressures. We've heard similar statements from those in jobs with similar levels of responsibility.

- The self-help remedies proposed seem designed to make us more worried as we try to find the time to take the suggested relaxing holidays, do exercises or find new leisure interests.

- Before believing that stress is worse now than ever before, compare yourself with your late-19th-century counterpart. You would have had classes of 50 to 60, wages dependent on pupils' results, the demands of a National Curriculum, awkward parents refusing to pay the compulsory fees and an annual inspection.

- The stress industry can seem like a growth area which encourages people to feel helpless because of even minor frustrations such as the photocopier being out of action.

Stress busting – a new interpretation

Should we believe the stress hype or the stress sceptics? To resolve the dilemma, we suggest differentiating states of stress as:

Distress → *Anxiety* → *Anticipation* → *Delight*

This will help you re-think your attitudes.

♦ The happy states of anticipation and delight are as much forms of stress as are the less happy ones of anxiety and distress.

♦ Each of these states will affect all of us at some time.

♦ Each is a necessary, and valuable, part of being human. It is not wrong, or bad for us, to be in any of these states.

♦ Every time we learn to cope with any of these states, we acquire skills that will enable improved handling of subsequent experiences.

♦ We can regard ourselves as being likely to have difficulty coping only if we face either multiple types of distress at the same time, or causes of distress over long periods.

♦ Learning to cope with any of these states can help you empathize with your pupils and be better able to offer them guidance on how to encounter change. Every day, pupils face the anxieties of new aspects of learning, being constantly assessed, having to work with incompatible companions and being required to produce assignments in media with which they are unfamiliar, while simultaneously battling with domestic difficulties.

'Should we believe the stress hype or the stress sceptics?'

Assessing your own distress, anxiety, anticipation and delight

♦ *Distress*
Continuous worrying, feeling sick, panic attacks, inability to act, sadness, waking in the early hours.

♦ *Anxiety*
Occasional worrying, working out every possibility before action.

♦ *Anticipation*
Stomach butterflies, rapid assessment of possibilities before action, looking forward to achievements, quiet excitement.

♦ *Delight*
Joyfulness, exhilaration, satisfaction with actions.

In which of the four states do you most often find yourself? To find out, tick your answers to the questions in Figure 5.

If you ticked mainly the first box in each answer, then you are experiencing 'delight' or 'anticipation'.

If you ticked mainly the second boxes, you are experiencing 'anxiety' or 'distress'.

Did your answers agree for the most part with those given by the school and college colleagues we surveyed for this book? Their answers are given below for comparison with your own.

Our sample of 42 colleagues consisted of those whom media-hype expects to be suffering anxiety and distress: 19 headteachers and deputies, 17 middle managers (e.g. heads of departments, key stage

1. When you first wake in the morning during term time, do you feel:
   immediately alert?
   or still tired?

2. Do you:
   thoroughly enjoy negotiations and discussions with work colleagues?
   or find you quickly lose patience with them?

3. Do you:
   relish your reading and lesson preparation?
   or find it hard to concentrate on them, often needing to re-read?

4. Do you feel:
   exhilarated for no particular reason?
   or sad with little obvious cause?

5. Do you:
   get started without delay on your work tasks?
   or keep putting them off?

6. How would you regard a Friday afternoon coping with an unexpected double class when there is no supply teacher to cover a colleague's absence:
   as an exciting challenge?
   or as an unpleasant problem?

7. Are you:
   eating, drinking or smoking as usual?
   or have you increased any of these significantly in the last twelve months?

8. Do you sleep:
   soundly?
   or restlessly?

9. Do you:
   enjoy talking about your work to friends outside your school?
   or find that you are obsessive or frequently complaining about it?

10. Is your health:
    good?
    or are you suffering from symptoms you don't usually experience, such as regular headaches, irritable bowel, disinterest in sexual and personal relationships, feeling dizzy, difficult breathing, heart palpitations?

Figure 5. Assessing your stress.

co-ordinators) and six others, including inspectors and peripatetic teachers. They were all at an age to have family responsibilities, and all had given themselves the additional challenge of studying for higher degrees in their spare time.

Responses

1. Feelings on waking during term time

Immediately alert 19%
Still tired 69%
Others: in between the two; alert in summer, tired in winter or term end; tired at end of term only; tired initially then perk up 10%
No response 2%

2. Negotiations and discussions with work colleagues

Thoroughly enjoy 76%
Quickly lose patience 17%
Others 7%

3. Reading and lesson preparation

Relish it 42%
Hard to concentrate/often re-read 36%
Others: it gets less time than it should; most done in the holidays; don't relish it but can concentrate 7%
Not applicable/neither/both/no answer 15%

4. Feelings

Exhilarated for no particular reason 14%
Sad with little obvious cause 31%
Neither/both 43%
Not applicable/no answer 7%
Others: if depressed or elated, there is always a cause; I don't have mood swings – sometimes get bright ideas 5%

5. Getting started on work tasks

Without delay 48%
Keep putting them off 42%
Both 10%

6. Response to the prospect of a Friday afternoon coping with an unexpected double class when there is no supply teacher to cover a colleague's absence

An exciting challenge 17%
Unpleasant problem 50%
Others: depends on the previous challenges of the week/on the class; I would consider this as part of what one would do for a colleague – a favour to be returned; as a professional, I would accept it; it's just normal; just a nuisance/inconvenience; light relief 21%
Not applicable/not answered/this could never happen in my school 12%

7. Eating, drinking or smoking

As usual 73%
Significant increase in the last twelve months 21%
Others: I have stopped smoking and reduced drinking and started eating to compensate 6%

8. Sleep patterns

Sound 64%
Restless 31%
Both 5%

9. Talking about your work to friends outside your school

Enjoy it 48%
Obsessive/frequently complain about 24%
Don't talk about it 20%
Others: both; Normal amount of teacher talk and gentle moaning 8%

10. Your health

Good 67%
Symptoms not usually experienced 33%
Irritable bowel (2); tearful and tired (1); stomach (1); skin problems (1); headaches (1); heart palpitations (1)

From the survey we learnt that our sample of teachers appeared to have fewer symptoms of distress and anxiety than media-hype led us to expect. We also found that many had causes for anticipation and delight. This is not to minimize the stress so often perceived in teaching. We are trying instead to show that all is not doom and gloom.

How are you coping with your distress, anxiety, anticipation and delight?

Answer the questions below to find out. The figures are the answers from our research sample so you can compare yourself with them immediately.

1. How many hours per week do you estimate you work during term time?

0–34	1%
35–39	5%
40–44	17%
45–49	10%
50+	67%

2. How many weeks per year do you estimate that you spend during school holiday periods without undertaking any lesson preparation or administration/management for work activities? (Do not include in this any time spent 'reflecting' on work.)

less than 1	2%
1	0%
2	22%
3	14%
4	24%
5+	36%
Not applicable	2%

3. Do you consider that you have had situations in your personal life during the last three years with which you have had difficulty coping or which have caused you to feel seriously distressed?

Yes	60%
No	31%
Not answered	9%

4. With which of these challenges have you had to cope during the past three years at work?

Incompetent/difficult subordinates	83%
Individual pupils with major social/ psychological/learning difficulties	80%
Particular class or year groups which were difficult to teach	69%
Very demanding/difficult parents of pupils at your school	69%
Inspection	67%
Classes of more than 25 pupils	64%
Unrealistic deadlines	57%
Activities for which you were not trained	48%
Financial difficulties	42%
Activities you felt were beyond the responsibilities for which you were paid	40%
Failure to gain a desired promotion/new post	36%
Serious conflict with colleagues or governors	36%
A bullying boss	26%
Activities you felt were beyond your competence	19%
No response	5%

Some of our respondents listed other distressing or anxiety-inducing factors. These included job insecurity through being on fixed-term contracts, taking on new posts, supporting supply teachers, lack of support from local authorities and social service agencies, too much marking and poor accommodation.

5. How much sick-leave have you taken, in the last three years which you consider was caused by your feeling unable to cope with factors such as those listed in Q.4?

Seventy-nine per cent of our sample had taken no sick leave for any reason. The remainder did not consider that their illnesses had been related to anxiety or to distress.

6a. What are your principal leisure activities (i.e. not related to work or family responsibilities)?

6b. How much time per week do you estimate you spend on leisure activities?

See Figure 6.

The few comments on this question demonstrated extreme contrasts from 'I have nothing like enough' or 'None at all', to 'I do 5–6 hours per week fitness classes plus I have all my weekends for leisure'. There appeared to be little relationship between hours spent working and hours spent on leisure. Of those who worked the longest hours, some also played for long hours while others claimed to have little leisure time. Nor did leisure time appear to alter greatly if the respondents were senior rather than middle managers.

The range of leisure activities of the sample is an interesting indicator of teachers' interests. Any of them can:

♦ give you at least temporary respite from distress;

♦ reduce or remove anxieties;

Figure 6. Answers to 6a and 6b.

Research sample grouped by numbers of leisure interests	No. of respondents	% of total sample	Average time on leisure	% of the respondents in each leisure group working 50+ hours per week	% of respondents in each leisure group who are not senior managers
None	3	7	None	100	66
One	6	14	6 hr 40 min	50	50
Several	31	74	11 hr 12 min	68	61
No response	2	5	No response		

♦ offer pleasurable anticipation;
♦ provide the delight of success.

Do they accord with your interests? (The numbers in brackets are those in the sample who listed each leisure pursuit.)

Arts

Film (2); photography (1); singing (1); theatre (4).

The social set

Eating out (4); pub (2); socializing (4).

Out and about

Aircraft spotting (1); birdwatching (1); charity/church work (2); sunbathing (1); travel/holidays (6); window shopping (1).

Sports

Cricket (1); cycling and motor-cycling (4); football (2); general (3); gym (1); hockey (1); keep-fit (4); sailing (2); skiing (1); swimming (6); tennis (3); volleyball (1); walking (11); watching ice hockey (1); water-skiing (1); weight training (1); yoga (1).

Home focus

Cookery (1); construction (1); gardening (9); Internet (1); listening to music (1); reading (8); studying (2); television (5).

Helping yourself to cope with distress, anxiety, anticipation and delight

Get the mind-set right

Always tell yourself you can cope, and reward yourself when you do.

Don't expect too much of yourself. You cannot simultaneously be the perfect teacher and school manager as well as, for example, an outstanding partner, parent, child, home decorator, sportsperson, singer and socialite. You will achieve all of these at some time in your life, but you'll need to select one at a time as your priority.

Accept that you won't always succeed, but realize that neither does anyone else.

Distress, anxiety, anticipation and delight all help you to diet, to cope with pain and to think more efficiently. How does this happen? Our physical responses to these four states include moving the blood usually used for digestion to our muscles and lungs; our saliva production decreases and our mouths go dry – all these discourage eating. Meanwhile, we release endorphins which reduce sensitivity to bruising (and possibly to bruised feelings). Extra hormones sharpen the brain to think of how to deal with problems.

Tell yourself you have coped before and that you will do so again.

Ask yourself what is the worst failure you can imagine; it's usually not that bad, so give it a go.

Be pleased when you successfully complete a task that was worrying you.

Strategies that offset distress and anxiety with anticipation and delight

Personal strategies

- Keep either Saturday or Sunday completely free of school issues.

- Cat-nap.

- Stroke the cat, dog, partner or children.

- Plan something you look forward to, whether it is a weekend meal out or pot-holing.

- Undertake exercise that requires both mental concentration and physical activity.

- Trust yourself and be optimistic.

- Praise yourself for what you have achieved rather than remembering what has not been done.

Personal work strategies

- Think positively. Isn't it great to have such a varied job that so immediately improves the achievements of others?

- When faced with an overwhelming pile of 'to do' items, first select something you *want* to do, not necessarily the most urgent or important as demanded by others.

- Set a limit to the amount of time you will devote to an activity.

Getting Organized

- Break at lunchtime, read some real rubbish, go for a walk.

- Freely express your emotions – both positive and negative.

- Don't expect too much of yourself; if, for example, you gave yourself a target of finishing the new class-room display by 4.30 and you had to leave it to be completed the following morning, was this really failure? You have achieved a degree of success and can anticipate the pleasure of completion the following day.

Classroom and colleague organizational strategies

- Classroom assistants could mark work and only refer to the teacher those pupils whose work indicates that they need particular guidance. In secondary schools, some self-marking, or group marking, could be organized.

- Use classroom assistants, or older pupils, to help young ones with, for example, clothing at the beginning and end of each day, so that you do not have to do it.

- Break down problems into manageable sections and deal with one at a time.

- Pace yourself – decide what is achievable in the time available and then add a little bit more in order to challenge yourself.

♦ For high risk takers: suggest to your head of department, curriculum co-ordinator or head teacher that
meetings might be cancelled for one week/term/
year. If your idea is accepted, reflect on what hap-
pened, or did not happen, as a result. Can written
memos or emails be substituted for meetings?
Alternatively, suggest a change in the times for
meetings so they are not held after school but,
instead, are held one morning per week before
teaching starts.

Helping your colleagues to cope with distress, anxiety, anticipation and delight

Get the mind-set right

Praise your colleagues (superiors and subordinates) for
their achievements. This includes praise for those who
cope with anxiety and distress. Sincere, brief remarks
and gestures can be made both individually and in
group meetings. This is important because teachers
spend most of their time with children from whom
they get various types of feedback, but they also
need praise from other adults.

Encourage colleagues to share their emotions; join
in their happiness or provide a shoulder to cry on. Such
sessions release tensions.

Humour helps. Everyone has to take the demands
on school seriously, but it is important to feel able to
joke about league tables, action plans, etc., without fear
of criticism for being light-hearted.

Strategies that offset distress and anxiety with anticipation and delight

Distress and anxiety can arise when you and/or colleagues are expected to take on new tasks or alter established routines. How can you help colleagues to convert that to, at least, anticipation? Consider these examples:

♦ Your school has always had termly boarders, but now there is demand to be met from pupils needing occasional overnight accommodation, so the head of boarding has to be more flexible.

♦ The school front office is to be redesigned, so that it looks more welcoming to parents, but the new, open-plan situation makes the reception staff feel exposed.

♦ It has been proposed that pupils should be streamed according to 'general' academic abilities as measured by achievements in the core subjects of the National Curriculum. You are delighted since your subjects will benefit but others are less enthusiastic.

♦ Two new pupils join one of your classes: one pupil is seriously learning-impaired and the other has limited vision. You are worried whether or not you have the necessary skills to cope.

These are just a few of the types of changes with which school staff must cope. Each of them can be seen as an opportunity for anticipation and delight, but the initial reaction is more likely to be a groan at the extra work involved. The challenge is to prevent the groan becoming a long-drawn-out sigh. For this, try some of these suggestions.

Understand why you/your colleagues are feeling distressed

Their attitudes will be one of these.

♦ 'It's new – I could gain or lose work, money, status, authority.'

♦ 'I am afraid I don't have the skills to adapt to it.'

♦ 'I don't know how to deal with it – people might laugh at my failure.'

♦ 'I'm cross because it's been imposed on us and no one asked me if I wanted it.'

♦ 'It's just another change in endless change.'

When you are aware of which of these feelings is dominant, if you are in school leadership, you can devise strategies to eliminate them as far as possible and/or provide emotional support; if you are a colleague, or subordinate, show that you empathize or sympathize. Are there ways in which you can offer practical assistance?

Involve the activists first

Every management text will repeat the mantra that the more everyone has participated in a change and its planning, the more delighted the whole school will be about it. We haven't, however, yet found a management text that speaks of the likely anxiety from 'democratic fatigue' or the attitude that, 'You take the decisions, just let me get on with my job – I don't want any more meetings'. So, don't try to involve everyone. What is more important and effective in helping colleagues feel pleased about change is to involve at the start the doers – not the doubters. Pick the enthusiastic types first.

Ensure everyone knows why a change has to happen

Spread information. Give time for people to talk through anxieties and frustrations. Set up e-mail chat lines and keep updating on progress.

Market the delights of change

Be enthusiastic – it's catching. Advertise how the change will benefit yourself and others.

Provide tools, time and training for change

Establish a 'one-at-a-time' achievement culture

Decide on the change priority. Work on and finish that one. With limited resources, you can't work successfully on all issues at once.

Value risk-taking

Be receptive to new ideas and initiatives. Offer opportunities to discuss them, even if it isn't possible to always go forward with them.

Welcome distress, anxiety, anticipation, and delight as naturally created mental workouts. It's the equivalent to creating a physical workout artificially by going to the gym.

'The general message is that if you want to get promoted quickly, it is better to follow a subject-based route, moving through schools or departments of increasing size.'

3

Career Management

With your time and stress under control, you are now in a good position to consider how to plan your career development. Start by checking out your career management to date. Have you followed the pattern below (or are you planning to)?

- *Year 1*: becoming known in your school; making others aware of your presence; enjoying the learning opportunities; enthusiastically participating in project management, e.g. school play, fieldtrips.

- *Year 2*: making your first promotion applications within your own school (primary or secondary); extending your range of project management opportunities to develop your career portfolio; beginning to attend short courses outside your own school; starting to indicate that you want to be considered for fast-tracking to headship (with projected shortages in the early 2000s, you should stand a good chance of rapid promotion).

- *Years 3 and 4*: first promotions achieved/applications outside your own school; professional development through a planned programme of regular short courses; becoming an active member of your subject or professional association; starting a postgraduate degree.

- *Year 5*: decision time; undertake your National Professional Qualification for Headship.

Beyond Year 5, what route should you follow? To answer this, consider the career portfolio you want to build.

Building your career portfolio

Careers used to be seen only as linear. You went straight upwards from classroom teacher to headteacher, and any deviation was not well regarded. Now there is a wider view. What you are trying to build is a portfolio of experiences. It's still true that it may enhance your promotion chances if these experiences are grouped around a major 'line of interest', but moving across 'lines' shows the width of your abilities. This is likely to be prized since schools have had to become more responsive to their communities and to pupils' needs for wider preparation for the changing work and leisure markets of their futures.

Your career portfolio – which line(s) do you most want to follow?

♦ *Management*: subject leadership; student welfare; middle management to senior leadership.

♦ *Leader of other teachers' learning*: advanced skills' teacher; professional development tutor; teaching on courses organized by your local education authority or local university.

♦ *Career break for family developments*: involvement in children's activities as, for example, playgroup/ sports leader; upgrading your qualifications; participating in elderly relatives' activities; giving adult education and management experience, e.g. in charity/voluntary societies; school governorship or board membership; self-employed tutoring; school inspections; examining and marking.

♦ *Alternative teaching*: special needs; teaching abroad; moving from the independent sector to the maintained sector or vice versa.

♦ *Union representation*: this is usually voluntary and within your own school initially. You may then choose to move to regional or national level. Union representation, even at school level, rarely combines with concurrent promotion in other spheres.

♦ *International experience*: short term (up to one year), e.g. for Europe, use the Central Bureau, for the Commonwealth, use the League for the Exchange of Commonwealth Teachers (addresses of these and other organizations are in the Useful Addresses section). Longer term, e.g. teaching English as a foreign language, contracts with overseas' development departments of government ministries, voluntary service overseas, permanent employment with international, and independent schools or with Service Children's schools – see the education press. Check before you go – will your school hold your job for you? Can you have it back at the same rate of pay and conditions as you have now? Are your teaching qualifications accepted in your intended destination (most countries do accept British qualifications but many have registration requirements so ensure that you are at least registered with the General Teaching Council in England or Scotland before you travel outside the UK).

Once you have selected your line(s), the next stage is to assess your abilities to get to where you want to go.

Which of your abilities make your promotion most likely?

From the list in Figure 7, select the four characteristics which you think are most likely and least likely to gain you promotion in your own or other schools.

Now compare your answers with those below which we obtained from a small pilot survey we conducted. We asked senior school managers their views on which of the above characteristics most influenced their choices of which staff to promote, either from existing staff or from outside applicants.

Characteristics	Your top and bottom four
Administrative/managerial ability	
Personal/social contacts with those who can influence promotion	
Knowledge of government policies	
Subject expertise	
Flexibility/variety in teaching methods	
Strong personality	
Good relationships with staff	
Willingness to co-operate to meet such requirements as OFSTED, TQA assessments	
Good appraisals	
Experience in a variety of schools/colleges	
Length of service	
Concern for pupils' welfare	
Holding/studying for a higher degree	
Holding/studying for a specialist qualification, e.g. for headship, for special needs, etc.	

Characteristics	Your top and bottom four
Ability to control pupils	
Conformity with/support for views of the school/college hierarchy	
Good relations with the headteacher and other senior staff	
Good relations with governors	
Leadership attributes	
Participation in extra-curricular activities	
Being innovative	
Pupils achieve good examination results	
Being in a shortage subject area	
Others – please specify	

Figure 7. Rating your abilities for career progression.

Getting promoted: adopt the right attributes

Most important

- leadership attributes

- being innovative

- exhibiting administrative and managerial abilities
- having subject expertise.

Rated as second most important attributes

- concern for student welfare
- strong personality
- studying for higher degrees or specialist qualifications
- participation in extra-curricular activities
- flexible teaching methods
- pupils getting good examination results.

Least important

- personal/social contacts with those who could influence promotion
- knowledge of government policies
- good relations with governors
- being in a shortage subject area.

The group we consulted consisted of those most influential in school promotions (11 headteachers from secondary schools; six headteachers from primary schools; two headteachers from special schools; one headteacher, a deputy head teacher and a housemaster from independent schools, and six others – deputy headteachers, department heads, subject leaders). All had significant years of experience, including making staff appointments.

Getting Organized

The sample was not large enough to work out if there were significant relationships between respondents' views and their types of schools, but the views did not vary greatly whatever the schools or colleges concerned.

- Primary, secondary and special school headteachers were equally likely to rate subject knowledge and studying for higher degrees as important.

- Primary headteachers rated concern for pupils' welfare slightly more highly than did secondary headteachers.

- Secondary headteachers rated abilities to control pupils, and to produce pupils with good examination results slightly more highly than primary headteachers.

Survey respondents were asked to suggest further characteristics which they thought important to promotion chances. Their additions were: luck, good timing, excellent teaching, influence in the staffroom and knowledge of how pupils learn. How significantly would you rate these?

For readers aiming to become headteachers, it is worth considering the added attributes deemed vital for those wanting top posts. Headteachers should be:

- visionary

- good communicators, approachable, ready to listen

- fair, instilling discipline, concerned to achieve equity

- motivators for staff

- up-to-date with government policies

- primarily committed to internal school matters, with low priority accorded to a role in the local or national communities.

Which routes make your promotion most likely?

We reviewed the career paths of the 28 senior-school staff in the above survey, with the following results.

For promotions in primary schools

- Go for first promotion within three to four years of starting teaching.

- Expect to traverse two or three posts, over an average of five to ten years, in more than one school, before becoming a headteacher.

- Travel via subject leadership to deputy headship in small schools, then move to larger schools.

For promotions in secondary schools

- Go for first promotion within two years of starting teaching.

- Expect to traverse six posts, over an average of 11 years, before becoming headteacher.

- Travel via head of subject department (in a small department or small school) to head of a subject department (in a large department or large school) to head of faculty or sixth form, to deputy headteacher.

For promotions in independent schools

- ◆ Go for first promotion within four years of starting teaching.

- ◆ Expect to traverse six posts, over an average of 25 years.

- ◆ Travel via head of subject department to head of a house to deputy headteacher.

The general message is that if you want to get promoted quickly, it is better to follow a subject-based route, moving through schools or departments of increasing size. The few examples of our mini-survey group who took slightly longer to reach senior posts had non-standard career experiences. These included two or three years as LEA advisory teachers or in school posts carrying pastoral rather than subject responsibilities; two had taken career breaks for family reasons and restarted their careers from the bottom again after the breaks (as did one of the authors of this book); one had become headteacher of two schools overseas in early career but had not then attained the same position on return to the home country. Those in special education had posts in mainstream schools first and varied experiences in different types of special education.

There was one question our sample did not need to take into account in their past career movements, but which has become significant in recent years. Do you move only to schools/colleges which are high in the league tables? From the early 1990s, all schools in England and Wales have been given a position in national league tables based on their examination results; some other countries are adopting similar systems.

Schools which are low in the league tables, or which are deemed to be 'failing' and/or have been placed in 'special measures' with the threat of possible closure, find it hard to attract staff. Thus your chances of getting the post you want in such schools are higher than in the successful schools which will pull in many more applications. It's possible, however, that it may be difficult to move on from low-rated schools.

Our advice would be to go for the lower rated school if:

1. It has a lively, determined and supportive head-teacher and governors with clear policies likely to achieve improvements.

2. You don't intend to stay more than three years in that post (start applying for alternatives after two years).

3. The school roll is rising.

4. You feel you can help make a difference and that you will be credited with your achievements.

5. You want to work there.

6. You're applying for a headship.

Which of your characteristics make your promotion more difficult?

There is anecdotal, official and research evidence that it takes longer to get promoted if you are female, or non-white, or have a large number of children, or have no children, or are over 45, or are considered fat, ugly or unusually short, or have non-heterosexual tendencies, or too many heterosexual tendencies, or qualifications in PE, or extreme political views, or parents who were not teachers, or . . . .

The bad news is that this list seems to include anyone who is not white, male, of European origin and in a long-term partnership with 2.4 children. However, a great many teachers don't fit this pattern and the good news is also that equal opportunities legislation, shortage of teachers and headteachers and changing societal attitudes have alleviated the worst excesses of rejection based on factors unrelated to job performance. The bad news is that these developments have also been blamed for contrary effects; for example, since it became legally and societally allowed for men to be headteachers of girls' schools, the number of female headteachers has declined. Another example is the extension of parental leave, which could militate against employing those likely to have responsibilities for their own children.

So, what should we do about the inequities that are likely to inhibit promotion unfairly? Most of them are factors we can't change (such as our sex), or can only marginally alter (such as our weight). Most of them are factors that will subconsciously influence those who select teachers for promotion, though all will try not to be prejudiced. We all tend to select as our friends/ partners those who look and sound much like ourselves, the same is likely to apply when we are making staff appointments.

In response to this, we have three choices. Which is yours?

1. Moan about the unfairness of life. Refuse to apply for promotion on the grounds that 'I'll never get it because of my . . .'.

2. Be determined that people must accept you for what you are. Turn up for the interview in a droopy skirt with a mismatched top, bright green hair and a ring through the end of your nose, and tell the panel you favour pupil selection by ability (your interview is in a non-streamed, non-selective comprehensive school).

3. Adapt to the prevailing culture. Schools as organizations need conformists with a spirit of individualism. So wear that suit but with a bright, ethnic shirt. Demonstrate you can help pupils achieve good examination results but that you also have bright ideas for getting your politics pupils to act out a mock-legislature or for the incorporation of artistic creativity into primary numeracy.

If you chose (2) or (3), you can increase your chances by gaining qualifications.

Which qualifications make your promotion most likely?

Personal

University opportunities

Post-graduate certificates, diplomas and degrees, i.e. a Masters, a professional doctorate (EdD) or a research doctorate (PhD) always aid promotion. Distance learning and part-time degrees are now commonly offered that make it possible to combine work and studying.

Which course?

If you are still in your early years of teaching, then opt for subject enhancement or teaching skills improvement (e.g. Masters degrees in Chemistry or in Learning and Development). Beyond your first promotion or after five years, consider management qualifications (e.g. MBA, EdD in Educational Leadership).

Guidance and finance

Use your appraisal interview to discuss possibilities. Your school may be willing to fund courses related to its individual needs. Therefore, find out school priorities from the development plan and ask to attend courses that will help the school with these objectives. Most university courses expect you to produce assignments related to your school's needs, so you can offer your school your services as a 'consultant'. Accept that you may have to pay for your own qualifications since you are improving your chances of moving on from your original school; banks offer career loans and most university fees for a part-time, post-graduate degree course, are less than the cost of one annual family holiday.

Government

Government-financed qualification opportunities alter frequently according to political priorities, so watch the education press and your staff-room noticeboard. Government funding will cover fees, and also sometimes provides for substitute staff to cover your absence on courses. Universities may recognize some courses as providing exemption from parts of Masters degrees.

Examples (England and Wales)

Management training

This list demonstrates the variety offered in the past 30 years; watch for changing opportunities in the next 30!

- 2003/4:   Headteachers' Induction Programme (HIP).

- 2001/2:   Staff College for aspiring and serving headteachers.

- 1998:   National professional qualifications for aspiring and serving headteachers.

- 1996:   Headlamp for newly appointed headteachers.

Getting Organized

- 1992: Mentoring for newly appointed head-teachers.

- 1980s: Diplomas and degrees on full-time secondment for aspiring headteachers, senior and middle managers.

- 1970s: One-term training opportunities for head-teachers and for departmental leaders.

Shortage subject training

Bursaries have been offered for basic training in, for example, technology, modern languages, and mathematics. Advanced skills in these, and other areas, may attract government funding.

Research funds

DFES grants from 1998 to help teachers to conduct and publish their own classroom research.

School opportunities for qualifications

Professional development days

Participate actively, offer to be a presenter.

In-school accredited courses

Schools now negotiate with local universities for courses provided by the school to be accredited as part of higher degrees or for teachers to gain credit for particular types of project management. Is this offered by your school?

School staff development policy

Does your school hold an Investors In People award, or similar? If so, they are committed to training you and it may be easier for you to obtain financial support for courses outside the school. Find out your school's staff development policy, how it awards finance and leave to attend courses and what courses other staff are attending. Get to know who holds the staff development budget; make them aware of your interest in self-improvement and be helpful to them in other ways.

Organization opportunities for qualifications

Unions, professional associations, local authority, school board, organizations of special schools, independent schools or faith schools, conference centres .... All these offer numerous short courses, some of which are accredited to qualification through a university.

Advantages:

♦ spreads your networking so that you meet those from other schools and areas who can help guide your promotion;

♦ courses tend to relate to the most recent developments, since these organizations can most quickly adapt what they offer to meet current needs;

♦ provide tasters so you can assess the direction you wish your career to take;

♦ require only short periods out of school and no long-term commitment.

Create a portfolio of both accredited and non-accredited courses, and of short and long courses. Select courses linked around only one or two career lines. Keep records of all courses attended – topics and outcomes – even including one-day courses.

Career planning?

All the commentary so far assumes that you are making career plans. Studies of promoted teachers indicate that most did have career plans. Studies of career decision-making, however, show uncertainty about the extent to which either you can direct your own career planning, or your choices are determined by circumstances, or are a mixture of both your choices and your situation.

We would advise adopting whichever approach best suits your personality and your circumstances. Drifters and risk-takers won't plan; the organized and risk-averse will plan; those who have to live in particular areas for family reasons will have plans made for them. Whichever way you follow, you need a mind-set that you *want* promotion.

Enhancing your promotion chances

Well, I don't really know. My degree result wasn't as good as I hoped, but I could have gone on for retail management if I'd really wanted, but I thought well – teaching – why not?
Student teacher, overheard in a school staffroom, responding to the question, 'What made you want to teach?'.

This potential teacher presumably did not envisage a teaching career, otherwise the comments would have followed our second tip on career management:

Sound, and look, positive about yourself, others and your school/college.

The rationale for this tip lies in recognizing that career management is not a once-a-year planning operation but is ongoing. Your attitudes, achievements and behaviour are being constantly (though usually subconsciously) evaluated by those colleagues who can influence your promotion prospects.

You may be lucky enough to have a formal and/or informal, mentor who is guiding your career. If so, take your mentor's advice and cultivate the contact.

Meanwhile, the rest is up to you. You are the only one who knows all that you have achieved, who has a vested interest in ensuring that it is known, and who will put it in the best light possible.

Tip

Career management needs:
- persistence (you are always selling yourself)
- personality (you are your main sales agent)
- presentation skills (you use these to demonstrate your abilities).

Keeping career records

Keep an account of *everything* you have done. Add activities to your CV as you do them. Then you have all the information ready for a job application. You won't have to dredge around in your memory for the date that you led the working party on relations with support staff, or for the years you taught Year 1 before moving to Year 3.

Select from your full CV the items important to the job for which you are applying. Demonstrate how your experience and abilities match what a particular school or college requests. Hence if a job description for a subject leader asks for the ability to demonstrate knowledge of Key Stage 2 requirements, then the first item in your supporting letter will stress that you have been teaching Year 6 and attending a training course for Key Stage 2. If the first request by the advertisers highlights the appointing school's need for good team workers, your supporting letter will begin with

'Find out your school's staff development policy, how it awards finance and leave to attend courses and what courses other staff are attending.'

how the team in your department operates, or how you participated in the team planning the school's centenary celebrations.

Mind the gaps. As you watch your career records grow, aim to achieve the most comprehensive experiences possible, especially if you want a headship. In primary schools, for example, try to teach all the Key Stages; in secondary schools, look for both pastoral and curriculum responsibilities.

If you don't already have career records, then start them now. Preferably, maintain them on a word processor for ease of updating, but file cards will do as well (keep one for each entry within the four areas below).

Your career – what to record

Basics

♦ Address. Phone. Fax. Email.

♦ Teacher's registration number.

♦ National Insurance number.

♦ Date of birth.

♦ Your schools, with dates of attendance.

♦ Qualifications – start with the highest level and the most recent, unless requested otherwise. For example degree(s), teacher training, A levels, GCSE; others such as first aid, life saving, health and safety, languages, etc. (all with dates, grades, awarding organizations – you will find it astonishing how many years after completing your own school education, you are still required to provide details of it).

♦ Referees – addresses, phone, fax, email – so you can contact them quickly when a job application is imminent; you must get their agreement to act as a referee and preferably send them a copy of your application.

♦ Personal interests – few schools now request information about these (perhaps they recognize that few teachers have time to continue with their personal interests!) but keep a record, especially if hobbies are relevant to school/college, e.g. you play a trumpet in a brass band.

Posts to date

Maintain this list in reverse chronological order and, unless an application form instructs otherwise, present the information in that order. For each of your jobs, record:

♦ School/college. Employing organization.

♦ Dates you were employed – make sure there are no unexplained gaps. If you were unemployed for a period, explain what you did, e.g. family career break, travel abroad.

♦ Title of your posts. Salary scale and salary.

♦ Brief description of the main responsibilities you held in each post.

Getting Organized

- Include part-time employment related to teaching, e.g. examination marking, private tutoring, leading adult education classes.

Professional development

This is all the formal and informal learning activities undertaken since your first appointment.

- All topics of in-house staff development days.

- Short courses attended, topics, dates.

- Qualifications in progress – keep a list of the subjects studied, titles of your dissertations and assignments. Any of these gives you a claim to expertise in an area that you may not have from your experience but will have from your studies.

- Experience of mentoring or being mentored.

- Membership of professional associations and examples of any involvement such as committee work or attending conferences.

- Publications – you can make a start on these through writing for your teachers' newsletter for your area, or for the magazines of your professional association.

- Voluntary/community activities, especially where related to teaching (e.g. being a school governor, running a youth club) or which demonstrate managerial competences (e.g. treasurer for the senior citizens' lunch club, secretary for the pub quiz league).

♦ Travel: include only travel for professional reasons (not holidays – but you can mention gap year experiences if you are relatively new to teaching).

Competences/experience

♦ Teaching – subjects and ages, examinations for which you have prepared candidates, examination results of your classes, teaching methods used and developed.

♦ Subject management, e.g. development work.

♦ Financial/resources management, e.g. do you have a budget for which you are responsible?

♦ People management, e.g. have you had to deploy classroom assistants, laboratory technicians or parents as helpers? Do you work in a team? What is your part in the team?

♦ Marketing/public relations management, e.g. working on the committee designing the school prospectus; meetings with parents; visiting feeder schools to encourage pupils to enrol at your school.

♦ Community relations, e.g. what is your personal involvement in local groups? Do you take your pupils to meet people in residential homes? Have you incorporated local people into your environment development programme?

Tip

Never send the same CV or supporting letter for different promotion applications. Adjust the focus, the prioritized details and how you stress your abilities to match the requirements of the job.

And finally ...

At what point do you become ready for career progression? Should you stay in teaching or move to allied professions? The last section helps you with these decisions.

4

Alternative Career Management

Ready to move on?

Use the following quiz (Figure 8) to assess your readiness to move on. For each question award yourself a score between 1 and 5, with 1 indicating total agreement, and 5 total disagreement. Score nil for questions you omit as unimportant or not applicable. The nearer your final score comes to 245, the more ready you are to change your career.

(Note: in the questions, family = those living with you/ dependent on you.)

How to move on

Leaving an established career for a new line of business is no longer the preserve of the career-break parent or a sign of failure: it's in line with current trends in the labour market.

Jobs for life are a past idea even in a profession like teaching, thought previously to be so secure. It's not unusual to have several careers during your working life. If you're interested in moving through different careers after only a few years in teaching, this isn't peculiar: see it instead as consciously planning to use all your different abilities.

Getting Organized

Circle your score

SECURITY FOR SELF AND FAMILY

Is the salary enough to meet your perceived
personal and family needs? 0...1...2...3...4...5

Is your housing adequate, safe, pleasant? 0...1...2...3...4...5

Are there schools/colleges nearby suited to
the needs of partners and other family
members? 0...1...2...3...4...5

Are there medical and care facilities nearby
suitable for family members? 0...1...2...3...4...5

Are there career opportunities nearby for
other family members? 0...1...2...3...4...5

Are your personal and occupational
environments physically and
environmentally safe? 0...1...2...3...4...5

Do you feel that your pension scheme will
provide adequately for your needs? 0...1...2...3...4...5

Are you on a permanent contract in
your main teaching job? 0...1...2...3...4...5

SOCIABILITY

Do you have strong ties/social links
in the area? 0...1...2...3...4...5

Does your family have strong ties/social
links in the area? 0...1...2...3...4...5

Does your main teaching job offer you:

 the scope you need to express
  your individuality? 0...1...2...3...4...5
 the amount of team working you enjoy? 0...1...2...3...4...5
 the social contacts you want? 0...1...2...3...4...5

If your teaching post does not provide
you with the sociability that you want,
is this adequately compensated for by family,
hobbies, voluntary work? 0...1...2...3...4...5

PRESENT CAREER ENVIRONMENT

In your current teaching post:

do the timetable and holiday arrangements
meet personal and family needs? 0...1...2...3...4...5

is there adequate opportunity for
your academic satisfaction? 0...1...2...3...4...5

are there enough professional
development opportunities for you? 0...1...2...3...4...5

do you like your immediate boss? 0...1...2...3...4...5

do you respect your immediate boss? 0...1...2...3...4...5

do you have enough 'perks', e.g. car pool,
free car parking, help with housing costs,
car loans, medical insurance? 0...1...2...3...4...5

do you believe in what your school
tries to do? 0...1...2...3...4...5

do you have satisfactory relationships
with colleagues? 0...1...2...3...4...5

If your teaching post does not provide you
with the career environment that you
want, is this adequately compensated for
by family, hobbies, voluntary work? 0...1...2...3...4...5

POLITICS

In your teaching post, do you have:

the degree of involvement in
decision-making that you want? 0...1...2...3...4...5

as much power/influence over
budgets as you want? 0...1...2...3...4...5

as much power/influence over other
staff as you want 0...1...2...3...4...5

as much freedom to take decisions
without referral to other staff as you
want? 0...1...2...3...4...5

as much opportunity to be guided
by other staff as you want? 0...1...2...3...4...5

If your teaching post does not provide
you with the political power/influence
you want, is this adequately compensated
for by activities in your family,
hobbies, voluntary work?   0...1...2...3...4...5

STATUS

In your teaching post, do you feel that your abilities and contributions
are recognized in your:

    Job title and grade?   0...1...2...3...4...5

    Salary?   0...1...2...3...4...5

    Office accommodation?   0...1...2...3...4...5

    Classroom accommodation?   0...1...2...3...4...5

    Parking space?   0...1...2...3...4...5

    Role at school and college public events? 0...1...2...3...4...5

    Rights to participate in extra professional
      events during school time?   0...1...2...3...4...5

    The respect accorded to you by students,
      colleagues, parents, superiors, governors? 0...1...2...3...4...5

    Opportunities for career enhancement
      or development?   0...1...2...3...4...5

Is there a satisfactory mechanism for
evaluation of status through,
e.g., appraisal, performance-related pay?   0...1...2...3...4...5

If your teaching post does not provide
you with the status you want, is this
adequately compensated for by family,
hobbies, voluntary work?   0...1...2...3...4...5

Are your family satisfied with your status
in your teaching post and other activities?   0...1...2...3...4...5

Are you now as well qualified as
your immediate superior?   0...1...2...3...4...5

TOTAL

Figure 8. Quiz.

Even ageism is gradually being reduced as a hindrance to starting new careers. The USA has pioneered the removal of compulsory retirement ages for university teachers – how soon will this idea cross the Atlantic?

If your answers to the opening quiz indicate that you're ready for a move, consider if you should be making this change right now by following through the steps to career change (Figure 9).

Where to move to

This section concerns careers that are outside teaching but still allied to education. Obviously, you could try any career, from nuclear scientist to pop star to refuse disposal operative or novelist, depending on your qualifications, abilities, interests and contacts. We're assuming that you are still interested in education, though not in mainstream teaching.

Start with the education press. In just one week in 1999, in Britain's main job sources, the *Guardian Education* section and *The Times Education Supplement*, there were plenty of alternatives to consider, including:

♦ literacy consultant

♦ web projects officer

♦ education at home tutor

♦ lecturers in teacher training

♦ LEA school admissions officer

♦ director for a watersports centre

Talk to your family
If your career change is going to affect them, how do they feel about it? Their support will be helpful.

Reassess your qualifications
Can they lead in a different direction? Are you still young enough to start a new career at the bottom? Can you cope with income reduction while training for higher rewards later? For example, with a maths, statistic or economics degree, how about becoming an actuary (pay on entry in 2000, £15,500–£23,000; up to three years' experience, £35,000–£55,000).

Get the mind-set right
You *can* do it. You *will* do it. It's *right* to do it.

Choose how to depart
1. Leave without another job in prospect.
2. Wait until an alternative application is successful or your own business is operational.
3. Check whether anything is likely to change at your school that might persuade you to stay, e.g. a new head, school reclassification or merger, pay rise. If so, will this overcome your frustrations in your current job?

Clarify your main reasons for leaving
Your new career *must* satisfy these. Do you want more money, greater job satisfaction, to meet personal/family needs or a new boss or organization?

Know the transferable skills you've acquired from teaching
Which of these are yours?
Making written and oral presentations.
Research, data analysis.
Managing and motivating groups.
Project planning, management and leadership.
Motivating colleagues.
Team-working.
Financial management.
IT support, advice, knowledge.
Coping with difficult customers.
Creativity.
Ability to work unsupervised.

Learn how to sell yourself to new employers or to prospective business partners or funders
Make your CV relevant and applicable to the job you want. Don't present it as a list of your teaching achievements.
Research the organization to which you are applying. Use any contacts you have.
Remember – it takes a seasoned interviewer no more than one to five minutes to decide if you are the

candidate for the job. Dress appropriately, walk, talk, sound and sit positively. Plan your body language.

Look at other people's business plans before presenting yours to the bank or other lender. Pay for professional advice. Attend a business course.

Assess your abilities and interests

Career analysis – through local or commercial careers advice services. List your personal and career history, your interests and attitudes, then do their aptitude tests. You will be interviewed on issues such as family and marital context, organization of work and home life, best and worst experiences of the past five years. There will be a detailed assessment of your strengths and weaknesses which can take a morning or several days. Expect to pay around £400 to £1,000 (2000 prices). *Life coaching* – a personal, life-skills coach to support and guide your self-help. The coach focuses you on what you want and how to get it. You are encouraged to empower yourself. The coach analyses you and sets stretching but realistic goals for a time period. Expect to pay at least £10 per half-hour (2000 prices) for telephone coaching, more if it's face-to-face. *Escape training* – a teacher sets up a course to help would-be escapees to reassess their lives, fantasize about their futures and evaluate leaving options. Look around for similar courses or start up a business in this area yourself.

Figure 9. Your steps to a career change.

Alternative Career Management

- teacher training jobs in private colleges
- leader for children's museum education
- head of professional studies in a LEA
- secretary to an Anglican education board
- discipline supervisor for a school in Qatar
- administrator for an adult education centre
- NVQ co-ordinator for a children's society
- education manager with the National Trust
- team leader for the Prince's Trust volunteers
- director for a young person's theatre group
- information services manager for a further education college
- professional assistant in an examinations board
- group leaders with children's adventure holidays
- management posts in English-teaching centres abroad
- recruitment consultant for education senior managers
- Director of Education for the Commonwealth Institute
- administrator/trainer for a European training organization
- examinations manager in an independent language school

- principal officer with the Qualifications and Curriculum Agency

- manager in the education department of the Institute of Physics

- tutor organizer for workplace learning in an adult education organization

- professional administrator and a regional organizer for major teachers' unions

- training and information manager for a charity helping children with speech difficulties

- consultant to deliver management development for team managers in Youth Offending Programmes.

There must be at least one of these you might try for – and each week produces different opportunities.

The agency route

While you're making up your mind, why not use the 'halfway house' of joining an agency for supply, relief or substitute teachers?

In the short term, this covers your financial needs during a career change-over, and it gives you the chance to experience different schools and responsibilities. This expands your CV and helps you to clarify if you really want to leave teaching.

In the long term, it's now possible to make agency work a full-time career. This can be either as a permanent supply teacher or through working for the agency itself as a manager.

Agencies operate within a seller's market. Schools increasingly outsource their teachers when:

♦ they need to cover maternity, sickness and parental leave

♦ budget deficits preclude employing full-time staff who need holiday pay and employment benefits in addition to salary

♦ shortage subject staff can't be replaced

♦ rolls unexpectedly rise

♦ there are more pupils interested in an examination subject than expected

♦ a school is in an unpopular location (the largest number of vacancies and the highest pay is in the London area; some agencies exclusively target particular regions only)

♦ specialists are needed (there are now agencies focused solely on, for example, special needs and modern languages).

The significant need for supply teachers can be guessed from the wording of agency advertisements:

'Get the right job this January! Choose your teaching position from over 200 vacancies ... Just turn up with your teaching certificate and CV and we'll do the rest.'

'To reward your expertise ... You can earn up to £100 per day. And we're the only agency that offers you a pension plan.'

If you don't want to teach at all, why not either launch a career in an established supply agency or set up a new one in your own specialism or area? The work would include placing teachers in long-term and short-term posts, liaising with schools concerning their vacancies, and interviewing applicants.

According to one advertisement for an agency manager, you'll need to be an independent self-starter, well organized, a team player, a good telephone communicator, flexible, friendly, empathetic, intuitive, diplomatic and, of course, 'in possession of a good sense of humour' (which seems to be a requirement of every education-allied job!).

Setting up your own business

While doing agency work, you can also set up your own business as a consultant. The part-time jobs then become part of your consultancy profile. Many who have left teaching follow this route. They add to their portfolios with school inspection, running school development days, participating as tutors on the government's schemes for training and retraining head-teachers, and management training for industry. There is a Society of Education Consultants in Britain which you can join.

Education consultancy is not well paid (around £250 to £1000 per day at 2002 prices, but this does not cover preparation time). Better rates emerge in management consultancy or project consultancy. These are harder to break into without commercial experience, but it's not impossible.

Personal businesses don't necessarily have to involve you in teaching. Why not market your teaching resources? Most of us have cupboards full of them. They need professionalizing from your egg boxes and sugar paper, but there are companies ready to help with this. They particularly seek out teachers' ideas, and you get around 5 per cent of the royalties. It's not a fortune, but it can add to your business portfolio. You might also be the one teacher who invents the school equivalent of *Trivial Pursuit* (for the cynics reading this, we don't mean the National Curriculum!).

Royalties also come from writing books or articles for professional newspapers or journals (but don't expect more than around £120 at 2002 prices). Being published has the bonus of making your name better known, and other consultancy jobs become easier to obtain.

Part-time tutoring outside schools is another useful addition *en route* to your new career, or as part of your new career package. Distance learning organizations need such staff. In addition to the long-established Open University, many other universities now offer similar courses, often to students abroad. Contact your local university to discover the possibilities.

Adult and further education offer you jobs in teaching everything from acrobatics to Zen. You can develop these from your personal leisure interests, but your teaching skills can be of direct use for courses in communications, languages, training classroom assistants, helping those with learning difficulties and in Adult Basic Education. Contact your local Governor Support Unit to see if you could teach school governors.

Examination invigilation is now on offer, adding to the more well-known setting and marking of examination papers. Schools and higher education institutions are now using externals for this rather than their more expensive full-time staff who need to progress the marking.

Will you jump or be pushed?

Are you or your school likely to become redundant? If so, will you go before, or after the inevitable?

Going afterwards gives you the certainty of a redundancy package and possibly free help from counselling or out-placement firms. Conversely, potential employers may see you as negative and reactive. Going before should give you a greater choice of jobs, and prospective employers should regard you as enterprising and positive.

However, your decision depends on the reasons for the redundancy. If, for example, your school is being merged or its type is being changed, then there can be some enhanced or alternative job prospects worth waiting for. If it is closing because of declining standards or numbers, the sooner you move, the better.

Is it easy to change careers?

No, but it isn't easy to stay in teaching if you don't like it. At the beginning of your new career, you will almost certainly:

1. Work longer hours than you did in teaching, though the timings will be more flexible.

2. Earn less than you did in teaching (plus you'll need to cover your own welfare benefits).

3. Veer widely from euphoria to terror.

4. Have to go out and market yourself aggressively, network continuously, chase up every contact and get used to telling people how fantastic you are.

Once you have made it through those early stages, you'll be able to assess if it's worth staying out of teaching. Your new career need not be permanent. It's possible to move in and out of teaching. Going back may be worthwhile if you've satisfied alternative ambitions, have not enjoyed the change, or if there are new opportunities in teaching.

Coming soon to a school or college near you ...

Consider the likely future opportunities in education. You may still decide to look for an alternative career – but it might be a new beginning in education. Schools might be abolished and replaced with home tutoring through electronic media. Lifelong learning may bring a much wider age range into schools. The post-1960s generation is the fastest growing, so educational provision for this group is an expanding field. The first years of university degrees are being franchised to schools. Changes in employment patterns are extending the school day and altering the pattern of the school year.

A recently developed school-related career is that of the bursar, or business manager. Self-managing schools, which have been emerging worldwide since the mid-1980s, need managers who relieve teaching staff of the commercial side of the operation. The business managers have responsibility for staffing, budgets, grounds, resourcing, sites and marketing, among others. Some teachers are transferring to this career route. There are bursars' professional associations for both the independent and state sectors. National training standards and an accreditation framework were established in 1998/9 and there is an MBA for school bursars from which some proceed to PhDs and EdDs. Business managers usually join their school's senior management teams, and some are designated as deputy headteachers.

5

Bibliography and Useful Addresses

Cains, R. A. and Brown, C. R. (1998a) 'Newly qualified teachers: a comparative analysis of perceptions held by B.Ed. and PGCE trained primary teachers of the level and frequency of stress experienced during the first year of teaching', *Educational Psychology*, **18**: 1, 97–110.

Cains, R. A. and Brown, C. R. (1998b) 'Newly qualified teachers: a comparison of perceptions held by primary and secondary teachers of their training routes and of their early experiences in post', *Educational Psychology*, **18**: 3, 341–52.

Caplan, G. (1964) *Principles of Preventive Psychiatry*, New York: Basic Books.

Carrington, P. (1999) *The Power of Letting Go: A Practical Approach to Relaxing the Pressure of Your Life*, Shaftesbury: Element.

Cooper, C. L. and Straw, A. (1998) (2nd edn) *Successful Stress Management in a Week*, London: Headway.

Covey, S. R., Merrill, A. R. and Merrill, R. R. (1997) *First Things First Every Day: Because Where You're Headed Is More Important Than How Fast You're Going*, London, New York: Simon and Schuster.

Dunham, J. (1992) (2nd edn) *Stress in Teaching*, London: Routledge.

Bibliography and Useful Addresses

Hicks, D. and Slaughter, R. (eds) (1998) *Future Education: World Yearbook of Education*, London: Kogan Page.

Hilsum, S. and Start, K. B. (1974) *Promotion and Careers in Teaching*, Slough: NFER Publishing.

Hodgkinson, P. (1998) 'The origins of a theory of career decision-making: a case study of hermeneutical research', *British Educational Research Journal*, **24**: 5, 557–72.

Hutchinson, F. (1996) *Educating Beyond Violent Futures*, London: Routledge.

Maclean, R. (1992) *Teachers: Careers and Promotion Patterns*, London: Falmer.

Moos, L., Mahony, P. and Reeves, J. (1998) 'What teachers, parents, governors and pupils want from their heads', in Macbeth, J. (ed.) *Effective School Leadership: Responding to Change*, London: Paul Chapman Publishing.

Newton, T., Handy, J. and Fineman, S. (1995) *Managing Stress: Emotion and Power at Work*, London: Sage.

O'Sullivan, F., Thody, A. M. and Wood, E. (2000) *From Bursar to School Business Manager*, London: Financial Times Publishing.

Peters, T. J. (1995) *The Pursuit of Wow! Every Person's Guide to Topsy-Turvey Times*, London: Macmillan.

Pollock, K. (1988) 'On the nature of social stress: production of a modern mythology', *Social Science and Medicine*, **26**: 381–92.

Thody, A. M. (1993) *Developing Your Career in Education Management*, Harlow: Longman.

Whitacker, P. (1997) *Primary Schools and the Future: Celebration, Challenges and Choices*, Buckingham: Open University Press.

Wilson, P. (1998) *Calm at Work*, London: Penguin.

Woodcock, M. (1982) *The Unblocked Manager*, Aldershot: Gower.

Useful addresses and phone numbers

Banks – usually have advice leaflets on setting up your own business and how to make and present a business plan in order to secure loans.

British Association for Counselling – advice on training and opportunities for counselling careers (tel: 01788 550899).

The British Council – 10, Spring Gardens, London, SW1A 2BN (tel: 020 7930 8466).

British Federation of Women Graduates – grants to complete degree studies – 4 Mandeville Courtyard, 142 Battersea Park Road, London SW11 4NB.

Business Link – advice on setting up your own business (tel: 0345 567765).

Career Guidance

Career Analysis Ltd – Career House, 90 Gloucester Place, London W1H 4BL (tel: 020 7935 5452).

Central Bureau for Educational Visits and Exchanges – 10 Spring Gardens, London SW1A 2BN (tel: 020 7389 4004).

Bibliography and Useful Addresses

Department for Education and Employment – Sanctuary Buildings, Great Smith Street, London SW1P 3BT (tel: 020 7925 5000, www.dfe.gov.uk).

Department of Education for Northern Ireland – Rathgael House, Balloo Road, Bangor, Co. Down BT19 7PR (tel: 01247 279279).

Government Departments – national, regional and local. Any of those concerned with employment offers lists of job placements, training and advice, counselling and placements

Ideas for Education – Hope Education – Orb Mill, Huddersfield Road, Oldham OL4 2ST. This company is interested in developing and marketing teachers' ideas for resources. They have an introductory pack, *Ideas Information* (tel: 0161 628 2788/0207/5957).

League for the Exchange of Commonwealth Teachers – Commonwealth House, 7 Lion Square, Tremadoc Road, London SW4 7NQ (tel: 020 7498 1101).

Learning Direct – they have details of courses all over the UK (tel: 0800 100900).

Local Education Authorities – ask your local office for a directory of adult and community education courses and for courses for retraining into other careers. These are often funded by government agencies, such as the European Union, and target employment minorities (e.g. minority ethnic groups, long-term unemployed, women).

Local Universities and Colleges – see your local telephone book for local courses.

Qualifications and Curriculum Authority – 29 Bolton Road, London W1Y 7PD (tel: 0207509 5555, www.qca.org.uk).

Scottish Office Education and Industry Department – Victoria Quay, Edinburgh EH6 6QQ (tel: 0131 556 8400).

Service Children's Education – HQ SCE (UK),Trenchard Lines, Upavon, Pewsey, Wiltshire SN9 6BE (tel: 01980 618244, www.army.mod.uk/army/press/family/schools.htm).

Teacher Placement Service – Understanding British Industry, c/o The Royal Mail, The Loft, 9 Howick Place, London SW1P 1AA (tel: 020 7592 8844).

Teacher Training Agency – Portland House, Stag Place, London SW1E 5TT (tel: 0207 925 3700, www.teach.tta.gov.uk).

Teacherline – a telephone counselling service, part funded by the DfEE (tel: 080 0562 561).

Teachers' Pension Agency – (tel: 01325 392929).

The Victoria League for Commonwealth Friendship – 55 Leinster Square, London W2 4PW (tel: 020 7243 2633).

Voluntary Service Overseas – 317 Putney Bridge Road, London SW15 2PN (tel: 020 8780 2266).

Welsh Office Education Department – Cathays Park, Cardiff CF1 3NQ (tel: 01222 825111).

Winston Churchill Memorial Trust – Travelling Fellowships – 15 Queen's Gate Terrace, London SW7 5PR.

Bibliography and Useful Addresses

John Wilson – runs short courses for teachers wanting to escape teaching (tel: 01736 797061).

Women In Management – helps to network and runs training and development seminars (tel: 020 7382 9978).

Women Returners' Network – offers advice to women wanting to return to employment outside the home and publish *Returning to Work*, a directory of education and training for women – 100 Park Village East, London NW1 3SR (tel: 020 7839 8188).